DOLPHINS ARE AWESOME

by Samantha S. Bell

12 STORY LIBRARY

www.12StoryLibrary.com

12-Story Library is an imprint of Bookstaves and Press Room Editions

Produced for 12-Story Library by Red Line Editorial

Photographs ©: Ricardo Canino/Shutterstock Images, cover, 1; Neirfy/Shutterstock Images, 4; guentermanaus/Shutterstock Images, 5; Willyam Bradberry/Shutterstock Images, 6, 17, 22, 24, 25, 29; Fiona Ayerst/Shutterstock Images, 7; Igor Zh./Shutterstock Images, 8; C Levers/Shutterstock Images, 9; Andrea Izzotti/Shutterstock Images, 10, 14, 26, 28; Jaros/Shutterstock Images, 11; VladGavriloff/Shutterstock Images, 12; Tory Kallman/Shutterstock Images, 13; VisionDive/Shutterstock Images, 15; Christian Musat/Shutterstock Images, 16; Selenit/Shutterstock Images, 18; Dennis van de Water/Shutterstock Images, 19; Timothy Craig Lubcke/Shutterstock Images, 20; Joost van Uffelen/Shutterstock Images, 21; Yann hubert/Shutterstock Images, 23; Jan Finsterbusch/Shutterstock Images, 27

Library of Congress Cataloging-in-Publication Data
A catalog record for this book is available from the Library of Congress
978-1-63235-434-1 (hardcover)
978-1-63235-502-7 (paperback)
978-1-62143-554-9 (ebook)

Printed in China
022017

Table of Contents

1 Dolphins Always Swim with a Buddy

Dolphins live in every ocean in the world, as well as some freshwater rivers. Hourglass dolphins live in the icy waters of the Antarctic.

Dolphins are found in all parts of the world.

Bottlenose dolphins are often found near the coast or continental shelf in warm, tropical waters. Pink dolphins live in the Amazon River.

Dolphins are social animals. They do not like to swim alone. They swim in groups called pods. Some pods are made up of mother dolphins and their babies. Others are made up of male and female juveniles. Grown males that are close in age swim together, too. Sometimes two males form an alliance. They may stay

TRAVELING WITH TUNA

Some dolphins travel with other sea creatures. Spinner dolphins are often found swimming with tuna. Scientists used to think they searched for food together. Now some believe tuna and dolphins help protect each other from predators.

The Amazon River dolphin is pink.

together for life. They act like best friends.

Pods are different sizes depending on the dolphin species. Bottlenose dolphins swim in pods of 2 to 15 dolphins. Striped dolphins form pods with 25 to 100 members. The dolphins in a pod hunt and play together. Some dolphins do not stay long in one pod. Others stay in the same pod for years.

Sometimes several pods join together. They can form a group of 1,000 or more dolphins. Some people have even seen megapods of more than 100,000 dolphins. These huge groups are made up of both male and female dolphins. They are usually found in open water.

40

Approximate number of dolphin species found throughout the world.

- Dolphins live in all the oceans of the world.
- Some species live in freshwater rivers.
- Dolphins form pods based on age, gender, or family relationships.
- The dolphins in a pod swim, hunt, and play together.

2

Dolphins Speak Their Own Language

When you are with friends or family, you communicate by talking, laughing, or even crying together. Dolphins communicate with one another, too. From the time they are born, dolphins make sounds, such as clicks, squawks, squeaks, and whistles. When they are above water, they use their blowholes to make sounds. When underwater, they make the sounds inside their heads.

Scientists are trying to figure out what dolphins talk about. The same sound can mean different things depending on what the dolphin is doing. A dolphin may squeak when playing or when hunting for fish. Dolphins make a sound called a burst pulse to chase away sharks. They use the same sound to correct a young dolphin.

Scientists are still learning how dolphins communicate with one another.

DOLPHIN NAMES

Scientists believe every bottlenose dolphin has its own special whistle. This signature whistle helps identify the dolphin in the same way humans use names to identify each other. Dolphins use their special whistles to let others in the pod know where they are. They also use them to stay in contact with other dolphins. Mother dolphins use their whistles to find their young.

2

Number of ways dolphins can make sounds.

- Dolphins make sounds when they play, hunt, fight, or are in danger.
- The meaning of a sound changes depending on what the dolphin is doing.
- Dolphins communicate using body language.
- Scientists are trying to understand what dolphins are saying.

Like people, dolphins communicate through body language. They might blow bubbles or touch each other's fins. Dolphins may slap their tails, bite, or nuzzle each other. A jaw clap on the water can mean a source of danger or food is nearby, or it may mean that it is time to move to a new location.

Sharks are dolphins' only natural predators.

THINK ABOUT IT

If dolphins used only sound to communicate, scientists might be able to figure out what they were saying. But they use body language, too. Why does that make it even harder for scientists to understand them?

3

Dolphins Swim Fast and Jump Faster

Dolphins have large, powerful tails with two flat flukes. The flukes act like underwater wings. When the flukes move up and down, they push the dolphin through the water.

A dolphin's speed often depends on where it lives. Dolphins near the shore usually eat slow-moving prey and do not need to move quickly to catch it. They can swim

Dolphins often spy-hop, or jump straight up out of the water to look around.

up to 10 miles per hour (16 km/h). Dolphins that feed on fast-moving fish in the open ocean can swim up to approximately 15 miles per hour (24 km/h). Scientists have clocked some dolphins swimming as fast as 25 miles per hour (40 km/h).

As dolphins swim, the drag force of the water slows them down. Air has less resistance, so to move faster, some dolphins "porpoise." They leap out of the water at regular intervals instead of swimming underwater.

It takes a lot of energy to swim. But dolphins conserve their energy when they can. They often swim behind boats, for example. The moving boats create a wake behind them. The dolphins use the wake for extra power. It helps them swim faster and farther without working as hard.

3

Number of miles per hour (4.8 km/h) a bottlenose dolphin typically swims.

- Dolphins use their tails to move through the water.
- Some dolphins can swim up to 25 miles per hour (40 km/h).
- Dolphins use their speed to catch prey.
- Porpoising helps reduce resistance.

4 Dolphins See under the Water and above It

Most dolphins have excellent eyesight under the water. They can see well above the water, too. Dolphins use their vision to capture prey and recognize other dolphins.

Because their eyes are on the sides of their heads, dolphins can see forward, to the side, and even to the back. A dolphin's eyes can also work independently of each other. A dolphin swimming on its side can look into the bright sunlight with one

Bottlenose dolphins can see very well underwater and above the surface of the water.

ELECTRIC DOLPHINS

Guiana dolphins live in murky water along the coasts of Central and South America. They cannot always see their prey because the water is too dark. These dolphins have special pores in their snouts. The pores help them sense electric fields given off by other animals.

7

Number of times better than humans dolphins can hear.

- A dolphin's eyes can adjust to looking above or below the water.
- Dolphins use their senses of sight, hearing, and touch to find prey.
- Dolphins can hear higher frequencies than humans can.
- Dolphins touch each other's sensitive skin to communicate.

eye while looking into the dark water with the other.

Dolphins have great hearing, too. They can hear a large range of frequencies and recognize small changes in pitch. The dolphin's teeth act as a kind of antenna to pick up sounds. The sounds go to the fat-filled spaces in the dolphin's lower jaw. From here, the sounds travel to the dolphin's inner ear. The dolphin also uses its large, smooth forehead, called its melon, to recognize sounds.

Dolphins are very sensitive to touch. The skin around a dolphin's eyes, snout, lower jaw, blowhole, and melon is as sensitive as the skin on a person's fingers and lips. Dolphins also use touch to communicate friendship. They brush up against one another and rub each other with their fins.

Dolphins have sensitive skin and often touch each other.

5 Dolphins Do Not Chew Their Food

Dolphins are carnivores, and they love to eat seafood. They usually eat 4 to 5 percent of their body weight in squid and fish every day. Species that live closer to shore also eat cuttlefish, eels, shrimp, and starfish.

Depending on the species, dolphins have 8 to 250 teeth. But they do not use them for chewing. Dolphins use their teeth to hold on to their prey. Then, they swallow it whole. If the

Bottlenose dolphins have 72 to 104 teeth.

Risso's dolphins often have many scars. Some come from being bitten by their main prey, squid.

fish is very large, the dolphin will rub it on the ocean floor to break it into smaller pieces.

Dolphins hunt for prey together. They also work together to catch it. A pod of dolphins will herd and surround a school of fish. Then, they take turns swimming into the center of the pod to catch the fish.

Bottlenose dolphins off the shore of Laguna, a city in Brazil, work together with people to catch their meals. Around the same time each year, a group of approximately 15 to 20 dolphins chase schools of mullet toward fisherfolk. Then, one of the dolphins signals the fisherfolk with a special head or tail slap. The fisherfolk throw their nets and catch the fish. The dolphins eat the fish that escape.

14

Maximum number of teeth a typical Risso's dolphin has.

- Dolphins eat fish and crustaceans.
- Dolphins swallow their food whole.
- Pods work together to catch their prey.
- Some dolphins work with people to catch fish, too.

THINK ABOUT IT

People and dolphins have been fishing together in Brazil for at least 120 years. Over the years, both the people and the dolphins have taught their offspring how to do it. But no one knows how it all began. How do you think it may have started?

6

Dolphins Have Built-In Radar

Dolphins hunt using a type of radar called echolocation. They use their large, round foreheads to make very short, high-pitched clicks. The sounds move through the water until they hit an object. This creates an echo that reflects back to the dolphin and is picked up by the animal's special hearing pathways.

Echolocation lets dolphins know the other animals and objects that are

Dolphins use echolocation to learn about objects and animals in their environment.

around them. They can figure out an object's size, position, and movement. They can tell the difference between an object made of plastic and an object made of metal. They can even listen to the clicks of another dolphin to find out what it is looking at.

Spotted dolphins are very good at communicating with each other.

Dolphins use echolocation as a kind of X-ray vision. The sounds dolphins make can move through some objects. When their echoes bounce back, the dolphins can figure out what is inside the objects. Spotted and bottlenose dolphins sometimes use echolocation in the sand at the bottom of the ocean. It helps them find fish hidden underneath.

219

Number of yards (200 m) echolocation from a bottlenose dolphin can travel.

- Dolphins use echolocation mainly for hunting and finding out what other objects are nearby.
- The sounds are created in the dolphin's melon.
- Dolphins hear the echoes as they reflect off of objects.

IN THE NAVY

Dolphins have worked for the US Navy for more than 50 years. They are trained to use echolocation to find underwater mines in deep or murky waters. Then, the navy disarms the mines. The dolphins also find equipment that is lost at sea.

7

Dolphins Sleep with One Eye Open

A dolphin uses its blowhole to breathe. But dolphins do not breathe automatically as people do. They must go to the surface to take a breath. If a dolphin fell asleep underwater, it would drown.

Sometimes a dolphin sleeps while swimming slowly next to another dolphin. Two males often swim side by side as they sleep. Females and juveniles may also pair off. A dolphin in a deep sleep does not swim at all.

Dolphins breathe through a blowhole in the top of their heads.

Instead, it floats at the surface like a log.

Bottlenose dolphins rest quietly in the water. While sleeping, they close one eye and shut down half of their brain. The half that is still working watches out for predators, such as bull, tiger, and great white sharks. It also tells the dolphin when to surface for fresh air. After approximately two hours, the two sides of the brain switch functions.

8

Number of hours a dolphin sleeps every day.

- Dolphins must come to the surface for air even when they sleep.
- Some dolphins sleep while swimming.
- Bottlenose dolphins sleep by resting one side of their brains at a time.
- Dolphins must always watch out for predators, such as sharks.

8

Dolphins Shed Their Skin

Dolphins are mammals, but they are not hairy or furry. In fact, they have just a few strands of hair when they are born. Instead, a dolphin's skin feels smooth and rubbery. Its outer layer of skin is approximately 10 to 20 times thicker than the skin of land mammals.

Just like people, dolphins have skin that is always peeling. New skin cells take the place of the old ones that flake off. But a dolphin's skin rubs

Dolphins' skin feels rubbery to touch.

10

Approximate number of hairs a newborn bottlenose dolphin has on its snout.

- A dolphin's outer layer of skin is thick and rubbery.
- The skin flakes and peels so fast that it is completely replaced every two hours.
- A dolphin's skin stays smooth and heals quickly.
- Blubber gives the dolphin its shape, stores calories, and keeps the dolphin warm.

off nine times faster than human skin. Every two hours, the outer layer of skin is completely replaced. This keeps the dolphin's body smooth so there is less resistance when swimming.

Underneath the outer layer is another layer of skin. It contains blood vessels and nerves. Underneath that is fat called blubber. Blubber helps give the dolphin its shape and keeps it warm. It also stores calories in case the food supply runs low.

NO DOCTOR VISITS

Sometimes, sharks bite dolphins, leaving huge gashes. But dolphins do not seem bothered by pain. In fact, dolphins heal very quickly. The wounds do not get infected. Some scientists believe dolphins' blubber has antibacterial properties. The tissue grows back, and the dolphins keep their shape. Only a scar is left.

Dolphins sometimes have scars on their skin from shark bites or boat collisions.

9

Dolphins Are Born with Belly Buttons

Like most mammals, an unborn dolphin gets nourishment through an umbilical cord. The dolphin grows inside its mother for 9 to 17 months, depending on the species. When it is time for her to give birth, the mother dolphin moves away from the pod.

Most calves are born tail first. The umbilical cord separates, and the calf has a belly button. The belly button is smooth and slick. The newborn calf can swim as soon as it

Dolphins are attentive mothers.

Dolphin calves stay with their mothers for many years.

comes out. It needs to breathe right away, so its mother pushes it to the surface. Then, the calf follows its mother everywhere she goes. It will not sleep for about a month.

The calf nurses from its mother for 11 months to two years. It may start eating some small fish when it is a few months old. But the baby will stay with its mother for three to eight years. A female dolphin may return to her mother or other female relatives to raise her own babies.

1

Number of offspring a dolphin usually has at a time.

- Dolphins have live births.
- A dolphin's belly button is smooth and slick.
- Newborn dolphins must take their first breath right away.
- A dolphin calf drinks its mother's milk for 11 months to 2 years.
- Dolphins stay with their mothers for 3 to 8 years.

10 Dolphins Are Great at Teaching Their Young

A calf has much to learn. Its mother teaches it how to swim, play, and go to the surface to breathe. It must also learn how to find food. The mother dolphin gives her calf instructions with chirping sounds. She shows it how to use echolocation to find fish. As she looks for food, the calf copies everything she does.

Other dolphins in the pod help teach the calf, too. The calf's older siblings often act like babysitters. This helps older dolphins learn how to be parents someday. Calves also spend

Dolphins teach their calves how to hunt for fish.

4

Approximate age of a dolphin when it becomes a babysitter.

- A dolphin calf copies everything its mother does.
- The mother shows her calf how to use echolocation.
- Other dolphins in the pod help teach the calves.
- Some dolphins teach their young to use tools.

FINDING MOM

A mother bottlenose dolphin will use her signature whistle more often in the weeks just before and after her calf is born. This helps the calf learn its mother's whistle. A few months after it is born, the calf practices a whistle of its own. If the mother and calf get separated, they whistle to find each other.

time with each other. The adults form a ring around them to protect them as they play.

Scientists have discovered that dolphins teach their babies to use tools. In Shark Bay in Western Australia, mother dolphins show their female calves how to hunt with sea sponges. The dolphins break off a piece of a sponge with their mouths in front of their snouts. They poke the sea floor with the sponges. This helps them stir up hidden fish. It also helps protect the dolphins from the poisonous spines of stonefish that hide in the sand.

Dolphins use tools, such as sea sponges.

11 Dolphins Are Playful, Fun-Loving Creatures

Dolphins are very playful, and mother dolphins often play with their babies. Scientists believe that playing helps the calves learn more about their environment. It also helps them improve their motor skills and practice behaviors they will use later. Play is a way for the calves to connect with other dolphins. They learn what they need to know to survive.

Grown dolphins jump, flip, and somersault for fun. They also chase each other as if they are playing tag. Dolphins use all kinds of objects for their games. One of their favorite toys is seaweed. They toss it and pass it around. They balance it on their tails and flippers. Dolphins play with coral, too. They swim with it in their mouths, and then drop it for another dolphin to catch.

Dolphins are known for their playful personalities.

Sometimes, dolphins play with seagulls.

2

Number of bubble rings a dolphin can make with its mouth one after the other.

- Playing helps dolphin calves learn survival skills.
- Dolphins play by jumping, flipping, and chasing each other.
- They play with objects in the water, such as seaweed, coral, and bubbles.
- Dolphins invent their own games and teach them to their young.

Dolphins also enjoy playing with bubbles. Sometimes, they make bubbles by smacking the water's surface. Other times, they form bubbles with their mouths.

Dolphins play with other animals, too. They swim under seagulls or pelicans floating on the water. They might pull out a feather or bop the birds into the air with their noses. They nip or poke puffer fish until they puff up. Some dolphins play with whales by riding on top of them. They will play with cats, dogs, and even people.

12

Dolphins Lend a Helping Fin

There are many stories about dolphins helping other dolphins. If one is hurt, the other dolphins in the pod push it to the surface to breathe. They swim beneath it, holding it up so it does not drown. They do not stop until the sick dolphin can take care of itself. Dolphins also fend off sharks together. If a dolphin is caught by people, other dolphins come to help it get free.

Dolphins also help other animals. A bottlenose dolphin in New Zealand helped two beached whales find their way back out to sea. When a lone seal pup near Mexico floated too close to the shore, dolphins helped nudge it back to the safety of the ocean. Dolphins have even rescued dogs that were too tired to swim.

Dolphins help people who are in trouble, too. Sometimes, they save

Dolphin and sea lion swimming together

Dolphins work together to fend off sharks.

people from shark attacks. When a surfer off the coast of California was attacked by a great white shark, bottlenose dolphins came to his rescue. The shark was biting the surfer's leg when the pod formed a protective ring around him. Dolphins also save people from drowning. When a 14-year-old boy fell off his father's boat in Italy, a local dolphin brought him to the surface.

4

Number of people saved from a great white shark by a group of dolphins off the coast of New Zealand in 2004.

- Dolphins help other dolphins in their pod.
- They stay with a sick dolphin until it is well again.
- Dolphins help other sea animals.
- Some dolphins help people in trouble.

STRANDED DOLPHINS

Sometimes a group of dolphins ends up on a beach. This is called stranding, and scientists are not sure how it happens. Some believe the group is trying to stay with a sick pod member that has moved into shallow water. As the tide goes out, the dolphins are stranded on the beach.

Fact Sheet

- Dolphins differ from porpoises in the shape of their mouths, teeth, dorsal fins, and bodies.
- A dolphin's life span ranges from 15 to 50 years. Orcas can live to be 70 or 80 years old.
- Orcas and pilot whales are actually dolphins. They all belong to the same family.
- Dolphins love to jump out of the water. They can jump up to 20 feet (6.1 m) high.
- Most dolphins have gray bodies with darker-gray backs and white or pink bellies. This helps camouflage them from prey and predators.
- Humans can detect five types of tastes. They are salty, sweet, bitter, sour, and umami, which is a meaty, savory taste. Dolphins can only detect salty tastes.

- Dolphins do not have a sense of smell. They use their sense of taste instead.
- Dolphins do not have a set of baby teeth and adult teeth. They have only one set of teeth their entire lives.

Glossary

alliance
A close relationship between two people, families, or animals for assistance and protection.

antibacterial
Something that fights against bacteria.

blowhole
A nostril in the top of the head of a whale or dolphin.

body language
Movements used as a means of expression.

carnivore
An animal that eats meat.

jaw clap
The loud sound made when a dolphin clamps its jaws together.

juvenile
A young dolphin.

motor skills
The movements of muscles to perform certain actions.

mullet
An ocean fish often caught for food.

prey
An animal that is hunted by other animals for food.

resistance
A force that slows something down.

wake
The path left by a ship moving through the water.

For More Information

Books

Carney, Elizabeth. *National Geographic Kids Everything Dolphins: Dolphin Facts, Photos, and Fun That Will Make You Flip.* Washington, DC: National Geographic Children's Books, 2012.

Rizzo, Johnna. *Oceans: Dolphins, Sharks, Penguins, and More!* Washington, DC: National Geographic Children's Books, 2010.

Simon, Seymour. *Dolphins.* New York: HarperCollins, 2011.

Index

About the Author

Samantha Bell lives with her family and lots of pets in the foothills of South Carolina. She loves writing about nature, and she is the author or illustrator of more than 60 books for children.